Published by Lulu and Bell
ISBN: 978-1-83990-300-7
Lulu and Bell 2023

"There are so many beautiful reasons to be happy."

Gratitude

Let's talk about gratitude and why it's so important for you. Gratitude is all about recognizing and appreciating the good things in your life. It's like having a thankful heart and acknowledging the kindness and support you receive from others. Practicing gratitude can bring a lot of benefits to your well-being and personal growth. Here's why it matters:

Boosting Your Happiness

Gratitude helps you feel more positive and reduces negative emotions like envy and stress. By focusing on what you're grateful for, you can shift your mindset towards optimism and contentment. This can make you happier overall and help you handle challenges with a better attitude.

Building Your Inner Strength

Being a teenager can be tough with all the changes and uncertainties. Gratitude helps you develop resilience by fostering a positive outlook. It encourages you to focus on your strengths and blessings instead of dwelling on the negatives. This can help you bounce back from difficulties and keep going, no matter what comes your way.

Strengthening Your Relationships

Expressing gratitude towards others strengthens your relationships and creates deeper connections. When you appreciate the people in your life, it makes them feel valued and loved. This builds strong bonds with your friends, family, and peers. Plus, it encourages kindness and empathy, making your relationships even more special.

Boosting Your Confidence

Gratitude plays a big role in boosting your self-esteem and self-worth. When you recognize the positive aspects of your life and appreciate your own strengths and achievements, it reinforces a sense of self-value. This can make you feel more confident, embrace your unique qualities, and navigate the ups and downs of your teenage years with a strong sense of self.

Finding Calm and Peace

Teenage life can be super hectic, with school pressures, social media, and everything else. Gratitude helps you slow down and be present in the moment. It shifts your focus from what you lack to what you have. This can reduce anxiety and bring a sense of peace and well-being into your life.

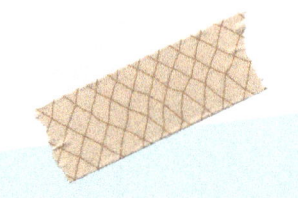

Embrace the power of gratitude! Cultivating a grateful mindset can bring you happiness, strength, better relationships, confidence, and a sense of calm. Take a moment each day to reflect on the good things in your life and express your gratitude. You'll be amazed at the positive impact it can have on your journey of becoming the incredible person you are meant to be.

"IT'S NOT HAPPINESS THAT BRINGS US GRATITUDE. IT'S GRATITUDE THAT BRINGS US HAPPINESS."

Mindfulness

Mindfulness is a practice that involves being fully present and aware of what is happening in the present moment without judgement. It means paying attention to your thoughts, feelings and sensations as they arise, without getting caught up in them or getting carried away by distractions.

Mindfulness can be particularly helpful in managing stress, improving focus and concentration and cultivating a sense of well-being.

Here are a few key aspects of mindfulness:

01.

Present moment awareness: Mindfulness encourages you to focus on the here and now. Instead of dwelling on the past or worrying about the future, it invites you to fully experience and appreciate what is happening in the present moment. This can help you feel more grounded and connected to yourself and your surroundings.

02.

Non-judgmental attitude: Mindfulness invites you to observe your thoughts, emotions, and experiences without judgment. It means accepting things as they are without labeling them as good or bad. This can help you develop self-compassion and reduce self-criticism, allowing you to respond to challenges with kindness and understanding.

03.

Mindful breathing: A common practice in mindfulness is to focus on your breath. Paying attention to your breath can help anchor your attention to the present moment and create a sense of calm. When your mind wanders, gently bring your attention back to the breath, without getting frustrated or discouraged.

04.

Body awareness: Mindfulness involves tuning into your body and becoming aware of physical sensations. By noticing how your body feels in different situations, you can learn to recognize signs of stress or tension. This awareness can help you take proactive steps to relax and take care of yourself.

05.

Cultivating gratitude: Mindfulness encourages you to appreciate the small things in life and develop a sense of gratitude. It involves noticing and savoring moments of joy, beauty, or kindness. By practicing gratitude, you can shift your focus from what may be going wrong to what is going well in your life.

Remember, mindfulness is a skill that takes practice. You can start by setting aside a few minutes each day to engage in mindful activities such as deep breathing, journaling, or simply observing your thoughts and sensations. Over time, with consistent practice, you can develop a greater sense of mindfulness and experience its benefits in your daily life.

"IN A WORLD FULL OF DOING, DOING, DOING, IT'S IMPORTANT TO TAKE A MOMENT TO JUST BREATHE, TO JUST BE."

Here are some mindfulness exercises for you to try

01. Breathing techniques can help you focus on the present moment and relax. Try the "4-7-8" technique this involves inhaling for a count of 4, holding the breath for a count of 7, and exhaling slowly for a count of 8. This exercise can help reduce stress and promote calmness.

02. Mindful Eating: Eat a meal or snack mindfully. Pay attention to the smells, flavors, and textures of the food, and eat slowly and without distractions. This exercise encourages mindful eating habits.

03. Take a walking meditation, take a slow and deliberate walk while focusing on your steps, sensations in your feet, and the environment around you. This exercise combines physical activity with mindfulness and can be done outdoors or indoors.

04. Listen to Music in a mindful way, choose a piece of music and close your eyes and listen attentively. Notice the different instruments, tones, lyrics and rhythms, allowing the music to flow through you without judgment or analysis.

Gratitude Journal

Write down three things you are grateful for today and why

Date

Write down three things that you appreciate about yourself and why

Gratitude Journal

Write down three things you are grateful for today and why

Date

Write down three things that you appreciate about yourself and why

Gratitude Journal

Write down three things you are grateful for today and why

Date

Write down three things that you appreciate about yourself and why

Gratitude Journal

Write down three things you are grateful for today and why

Date

Write down three things that you appreciate about yourself and why

Gratitude Journal

Write down three things you are grateful for today and why

Date

Write down three things that you appreciate about yourself and why

Gratitude Journal

Write down three things you are grateful for today and why

Date

Write down three things that you appreciate about yourself and why

Gratitude Journal

Write down three things you are grateful for today and why

Date

Write down three things that you appreciate about yourself and why

Gratitude Journal

Write down three things you are grateful for today and why

Date

Write down three things that you appreciate about yourself and why

Gratitude Journal

Write down three things you are grateful for today and why

Date

Write down three things that you appreciate about yourself and why

Gratitude Journal

Write down three things you are grateful for today and why

Date

Write down three things that you appreciate about yourself and why

Gratitude Journal

Write down three things you are grateful for today and why

Date

Write down three things that you appreciate about yourself and why

Gratitude Journal

Write down three things you are grateful for today and why

Date

Write down three things that you appreciate about yourself and why

Gratitude Journal

Write down three things you are grateful for today and why

Date

Write down three things that you appreciate about yourself and why

Gratitude Journal

Write down three things you are grateful for today and why

Date

Write down three things that you appreciate about yourself and why

Gratitude Journal

Write down three things you are grateful for today and why

Date

Write down three things that you appreciate about yourself and why

Gratitude Journal

Write down three things you are grateful for today and why

Date

Write down three things that you appreciate about yourself and why

Gratitude Journal

Write down three things you are grateful for today and why

Date

Write down three things that you appreciate about yourself and why

Gratitude Journal

Write down three things you are grateful for today and why

Date

Write down three things that you appreciate about yourself and why

Gratitude Journal

Write down three things you are grateful for today and why

Date

Write down three things that you appreciate about yourself and why

Gratitude Journal

Write down three things you are grateful for today and why

Date

Write down three things that you appreciate about yourself and why

Gratitude Journal

Write down three things you are grateful for today and why

Date

Write down three things that you appreciate about yourself and why

Gratitude Journal

Write down three things you are grateful for today and why

Date

List three things in your daily life that brings you joy or make you smile

Gratitude Journal

Write down three things you are grateful for today and why

Date

List three things in your daily life that brings you joy or make you smile

Gratitude Journal

Write down three things you are grateful for today and why

Date

List three things in your daily life that brings you joy or make you smile

Gratitude Journal

Write down three things you are grateful for today and why

Date

List three things in your daily life that brings you joy or make you smile

Gratitude Journal

Write down three things you are grateful for today and why

Date

List three things in your daily life that brings you joy or make you smile

Gratitude Journal

Write down three things you are grateful for today and why

Date

List three things in your daily life that brings you joy or make you smile

Gratitude Journal

Write down three things you are grateful for today and why

Date

List three things in your daily life that brings you joy or make you smile

Gratitude Journal

Write down three things you are grateful for today and why

Date

List three things in your daily life that brings you joy or make you smile

Gratitude Journal

Write down three things you are grateful for today and why

Date

List three things in your daily life that brings you joy or make you smile

Gratitude Journal

Write down three things you are grateful for today and why

Date

List three things in your daily life that brings you joy or make you smile

Gratitude Journal

Write down three things you are grateful for today and why

Date

List three things in your daily life that brings you joy or make you smile

Gratitude Journal

Write down three things you are grateful for today and why

Date

List three things in your daily life that brings you joy or make you smile

Gratitude Journal

Write down three things you are grateful for today and why

Date

List three things in your daily life that brings you joy or make you smile

Gratitude Journal

Write down three things you are grateful for today and why

Date

List three things in your daily life that brings you joy or make you smile

Gratitude Journal

Write down three things you are grateful for today and why

Date

List three things in your daily life that brings you joy or make you smile

Gratitude Journal

Write down three things you are grateful for today and why

Date

List three things in your daily life that brings you joy or make you smile

Gratitude Journal

Write down three things you are grateful for today and why

Date

List three things in your daily life that brings you joy or make you smile

Gratitude Journal

Write down three things you are grateful for today and why

Date

List three things in your daily life that brings you joy or make you smile

Gratitude Journal

Write down three things you are grateful for today and why

Date

List three things in your daily life that brings you joy or make you smile

Gratitude Journal

Write down three things you are grateful for today and why

Date

List three things in your daily life that brings you joy or make you smile

Gratitude Journal

Write down three things you are grateful for today and why

Date

List three things in your daily life that brings you joy or make you smile

"Know you worth. Don't ask for it. State it once and never accept anything less."

Affirmations

Affirmations are positive statements that you repeat to yourself regularly, intending to shift your mindset and beliefs. They are powerful tools that can help build self-confidence, improve your self-esteem, and cultivate a positive outlook on life. By practicing affirmations, you can create a mental environment that supports personal growth and well-being.

When you repeat positive statements about yourself, your abilities, or your circumstances, you begin to reprogram your subconscious mind. Over time, this repetition helps to counter negative self-talk, self-doubt, and limiting beliefs. Affirmations can help you develop a more optimistic mindset, increase your self-awareness, and foster a sense of empowerment.

To make the most of affirmations, keep the following tips in mind:

▶ Use positive language: Craft your affirmations using positive words and phrases. For example, instead of saying, "I am not afraid of failure," rephrase it as "I am confident in my ability to overcome challenges."

▶ Be specific and personal: Tailor affirmations to your own experiences and aspirations. This personalizes the statements and makes them more meaningful to you.

▶ Practice regularly: Set aside a few minutes each day to repeat your affirmations. You can say them out loud, write them down, or use digital tools like apps or reminders. Consistency is key to seeing positive changes.

▶ Believe in what you say: While initially, you might not fully believe the affirmations, approach them with an open mind and embrace the possibility that they can become true. Trust the process and be patient with yourself.

▶ Visualize success: As you repeat your affirmations, visualize yourself embodying the qualities or achieving the goals you're affirming. Engaging your imagination can enhance the effectiveness of the practice.

▶ Combine affirmations with action: While affirmations are a valuable tool, they work best when paired with intentional action. Take steps towards your goals, practice self-care, and surround yourself with positive influences.

Remember, affirmations are not a magical solution, but rather a tool to support your personal growth. They work in conjunction with other healthy habits and mindset shifts. By incorporating affirmations into your daily routine, you can develop a more positive and empowered mindset, which can have a profound impact on your well-being and success.

Become your own cheerleader

Gratitude Journal

Write down three things you are grateful for today and why

Date

List three affirmations

Gratitude Journal

Write down three things you are grateful for today and why

Date

List three affirmations

Gratitude Journal

Write down three things you are grateful for today and why

Date

List three affirmations

Gratitude Journal

Write down three things you are grateful for today and why

Date

List three affirmations

Gratitude Journal

Write down three things you are grateful for today and why

Date

List three affirmations

Gratitude Journal

Write down three things you are grateful for today and why

Date

List three affirmations

Gratitude Journal

Write down three things you are grateful for today and why

Date

List three affirmations

Gratitude Journal

Write down three things you are grateful for today and why

Date

List three affirmations

Gratitude Journal

Write down three things you are grateful for today and why

Date

List three affirmations

Gratitude Journal

Write down three things you are grateful for today and why

Date

List three affirmations

Gratitude Journal

Write down three things you are grateful for today and why

Date

List three affirmations

Gratitude Journal

Write down three things you are grateful for today and why

Date

List three affirmations

Ingram Content Group UK Ltd.
Milton Keynes UK
UKHW051138260523
422353UK00004B/56